Leslie Head

My Earthly Angel

AmErica House
Baltimore

Cover design: Patricia Wershiner

ISBN:1-893162-90-7
PUBLISHED BY
AMERICA HOUSE BOOK PUBLISHERS
www.ericahouse.com
Baltimore

Printed in the United States of America

To my husband and parents who offered an endless amount of support and encouragement to me throughout the book's completion and to my sister whose godly and loving spirit is the true inspiration for it

CHAPTER 1

The room was filled with wall-to-wall people. Balloons, banners, and streamers hung to add to the ambiance of the celebration. The couple across from me was in a world all of their own. Their faces close enough to feel each other's hot breath, totally unaware and uninterested in all the chaos and celebration that was going on around them. No doubt, whispering sweet nothings to each other. The group of girls to my left was anxiously listening to the details of the long awaited date with the school hunk.

People, with whom I grew up, shared a special kinship and mutual respect surrounded me. Yet, among all of my friends, among all of the laughter, among all of the talking and among all of the music, I felt alone. Life seemed to be happening around me. It was like life was moving in slow motion and I was forced to watch the joy and excitement and peace that other people were experiencing; something that I wanted desperately to experience for my own.

It was an all too familiar scene for me during my puberty years; feeling completely alone in a room full of people, feeling nothing but emptiness and despair in the midst of a vast array of love, laughter and friendships. I was growing hair in places I didn't want it. I was expanding in places I felt I didn't need it and I was three and four inches taller than everybody else around me. I felt inadequate, awkward and especially confused. I had no idea who I really was and didn't even like the person I thought I was. All of those emotions and feelings eventually drove me deeper and deeper into depression. There were even moments I experienced feelings of utter despair, wishing my life, as I had come to know and expect it, was over.

My incredibly supportive and loving family and my innate ability to act my way through those very miserable moments were the only things that made the days bearable. I often played out my life through my own hopes and dreams; disregarding reality and imagining for myself a different look, a different personality and a very different life. Romanticizing and fantasizing helped to create the escape I needed to survive through those moments.

When the situation or circumstance required it of me, I could turn off those horrifying and distressing feelings with the blink of an eye. Whether through the life I imagined in my own head or through the actress I became to those around me, the feelings of inadequacy, loneliness and emptiness I truly felt inside could disappear for a short period of time.

I was essentially living a double life. To those I

called my friends, I was anything but the picture of despair. Most people knew me to be confident, smart, assertive, friendly and funny. To those who knew me best, I was often self-conscious, shy, withdrawn and, sometimes, even depressed. Somewhere deep inside, I knew I was obviously capable of being the person that most people saw me to be, but, for the most part, it wasn't reflective of the real havoc my emotions were putting my heart and mind through. In a school full of complete strangers who I felt inferior to and intimidated by, I was shy and withdrawn.

In church, I found a safe haven. I could hide behind a façade of being friendly, confident and assertive. There, I even developed relationships with two other girls, whom I did everything with for the better part of my teenage years. All of our free moments, our sleepovers, our parties, all were spent together. We were inseparable, yet, they were both totally unaware of the deep seeded depression that I often reverted to in the privacy and protection of my home; the side that my family knew about all too well.

I accepted Jesus Christ as my Lord and Savior when I was only 10 years old. And at that time, I truly believed I was ready to take on all the emotional and spiritual responsibilities of being a Christian. I felt assured of and trusted in His unconditional love and understood that, as Christians, we were to give our lives over to Him. I understood the basic Christian principle that God promised to love me, forgive me and protect me.

I understood that He had set a special place for me in heaven and anxiously awaited my arrival. I thought I even understood that we, as Christians, should lay before Him all of our old physical and emotional feelings, changing who we are forever. With the development of those oppressive feelings I came face to face with how little I really understood. And it took me several more years to finally realize that turning over my life and my old self to Him was not just a surface decision. It was a deep, arduous gutting of self. It was a matter of turning over my fears, my doubts, all of my emotions to God and allowing Him to take control.

In 2 Corinthians 5:17 it says, "Therefore, if anyone is in Christ, he is a new creation, old things have passed away; behold, all things have become new." (Spirit Filled Life Bible) I grew up in the church. I had heard and memorized this verse more times than I can even count. It's such a simple concept presented by the apostle Paul. The very basic idea that Christ's death and resurrection and our identification with Him by faith, make existence as that new creation very real.

Even years after accepting God into my heart, I had yet to grasp that simple concept. Unconsciously, relinquishing control of all of those fears and self-doubt, was something I felt incapable of doing. That's the very thing we, as Christians, are instructed to do in 1 Peter 5:7

to " ...humble yourselves under the mighty hand of God, that He may exalt you in due time, casting all your care upon Him, for He cares for you." (Spirit Filled Life Bible)

He's a God who gave up His only Son to save us, who's willing to take on all of our problems. He's a God who loves us and protects us just the same. There is no other relationship in the world that can offer such selfless and generous acts. I spent so many wasted years trying to keep control of my seemingly horrific life, attempting to be what I thought others wanted me to be and disliking the very person I was portraying. When all along, God was willing to accept me for who I was, wanting me to love the person He created and for whom He was willing to sacrifice His Son.

The most unfortunate part of all this was the fact that I was blessed with one of the most loving and giving families I had ever had the experience of knowing. It took years before I came to totally appreciate this beautiful and inspirational family. Mine was a family that most people will never have the joy of experiencing and one that most people don't even know exists.

My mother was what I believed to be the perfect portrayal of the "virtuous wife" described in the book of Proverbs. She was blessed with an overabundance of wisdom and love. She was a supporter, an encourager and a friend. She taught me patience, kindness and respect. My father was an unbelievably generous and sensitive man. Such qualities are ones virtually unheard of in a man, but ones that were overwhelmingly evident in my father. He taught me the importance of being wise with my money, while never forgetting the importance of giving and sharing with what you had been blessed. The one member of our family, to whom I attribute most of what I am today, is my sister. She was the best of each of my parents; selfless, wise, giving, and caring. And it was her humble, compassionate and generous spirit, which taught me the true meaning of life and defined to me my role as a Christian. She became my inspiration, my role model, and always, my best friend.

My parents fulfilled every aspect of what God had intended for a parent. They showed me love; they gave me support, they taught me about the love of Jesus Christ. It was my sister, though, which played a significant part in the dramatic transformation of my life. My sister had such an impact on my life and it was because of who she was that inspired me to tell this story. It is a story that follows our lives together as sisters through some of the most difficult times that either of us had ever experienced and, through it all, my own personal struggle to find myself and to love that person God created me to be.

Although this story focuses on just a few brief chapters in my life, they are periods of time that brought about the most changes. Through my family's own loving and compassionate spirit, I was able to escape those reigns of depression as a young child. Through my sister's own struggles, she became my inspiration to be the full potential God intended for me to be.

It was a long and trying road to get where God wanted me but, in the end, I gained a whole new perspective on life. My sister was the inspiring testament of this new perspective on life and the joys and rewards of it. Not only did I once again see my sister as an inspiration, a best friend, a role model, but I also saw her as my earthly angel.

CHAPTER 2

Many years ago my sister presented a frame to me, with a beautiful inscription that read, " A sister listens with a heart and hears what is not being said." As we became older and more mature, my sister and I developed a very close relationship. And with such a close relationship came the joys and comforts of it.

Being best friends on top of being sisters gave us a special bond and gave us that insight into each other, which made her gift so meaningful and significant to the both of us. Most sisters, I believe, experience the kind of relationship where you could be the worst of enemies one-minute and the best of friends the next. And my sister and I experienced our fair share of that kind of relationship as little children. But as we grew older and before we developed the special bond we now both enjoy, our relationship began to take on a new level.

The coming of puberty not only brought the physical and emotional changes for me, but it started a new level to my relationship with my sister. For the most part, I was experiencing feelings that I am sure most teenagers feel at some point in time during the puberty years; ugliness, loneliness, sadness, shyness, awkwardness.

But for me, since these feelings dominated many of my thoughts, it also dominated much of my life. And it was those invasive thoughts, which made my life seem, at times, out of control and unbearable.

I can remember many nights where I just sat on my bed and cried, not always knowing exactly why and sometimes not really caring. A mere look in the mirror could set off what seemed like hours of depression. An angry look from a schoolmate could bring me to tears. An oral report could bring days of nausea. Though, like the adept actress I had become, I could turn off all of the emotions and turmoil that came with those moments. One minute I could be balled up on my bed in total despair, wishing life would just pass me by and, the next minute, I could have my friends doubled over with laughter.

I cannot even begin to imagine what it must have been like for my parents. Watching me cry, seeing me depressed, witnessing me being tormented by the most trivial things in life. Nothing they said or nothing they did seemed to do anything to alleviate the obvious treachery I considered my life. As a parent, I'm sure that was the most distressing situation to witness; a feeling of utter helplessness and frustration. They were forced to sit by and watch one of their children hurting, slowly realizing nothing they did would be the source of comfort that could ease the pain.

In a seemingly hopeless situation, I believe, my

parents only did what their instincts told them to do. It's an instinct instilled in most people. Compassion – a selfless and generous trait that takes over when you see someone hurting; your needs and feelings become inconsequential to better focus on the needs and feelings of those that are hurting. Without even realizing it, my parents' lives began to change its focus. Life gradually left the mundane routine that most people unconsciously fall into and turned into a life that was dependent upon how everything would affect me. "Would this make her feel better about herself?" "Would this make life a littler easier for her?"

Although I know their hearts were in the right place, I believe that the life that my parents had created for me had an unfortunate two-fold affect. At least 3 years of my life were spent in the forefront of my family's lives. It was a lifestyle, which involved a lot of sacrifices and a lot of patience on the part of the rest of my family. Life basically revolved around me, an environment created to make me comfortable.

What young teenager wouldn't bask in the glow of being the center of their world; having people sacrifice and manipulate to make sure they were happy and content, being first in their family's every thought and feeling, getting things their way and having people at their beck and call. At the time, I never realized it nor would ever admit it if I had, but the environment paved the road for me to becoming naturally selfish.

Webster's dictionary defines being selfish as "having such regard for one's own interests and advantage that the welfare of others becomes of less concern than is considered just". Such a short statement but one that indicates volumes about its owner. As a Christian, I was as far away from God as I could possibly be. I may have been having a Bible study. I may have never been rude to others. And I probably was always friendly, but nonetheless, I was not being obedient to God.

In 1 Peter 3:8, God calls us to be " ...of one mind, having compassion for one another, love as brothers, be tenderhearted, be courteous..." (Spirit Filled Life Bible). It was virtually impossible for me to have such compassion for others. My mind was so distorted and distracted by thoughts of the "me", my heart didn't have a chance to reach out with compassion to the world. And until I was able to allow God to guide my heart in that direction, I would never be where God wanted me to be and, as a result, never experience the grace and mercy He offers through obedience to Him.

Even entering into adulthood, anxious to take my first few steps out into the real world, I would feel the affects of my selfishness. My world for so long had been padded, protected and gently guided by my loving family. Now, I was trying to step out on my own in the, at times, harsh, cruel world and quickly came to realize how cushioned my life had been and how totally unprepared I was to be an integral part of it. Even then, after many falls and many trials, I still could not grasp the significance of my difficulty melding into the real world and I eventually began to experience a new kind of sorrow and frustration somewhat like the feelings I experienced as a young girl.

And although I didn't vent the frustration and grief all through tears, I vented it just the same. Anger and bitterness, at times, overcame my heart, further destroying any hope of becoming who God wanted me to be. I was completely blind to my own selfishness and its cause of the new kind of feelings I was experiencing. As an adult, I had to take responsibility for my own actions. My parents might have created the atmosphere for the development of such a situation, though, the blame laid solely on my own inability to recognize it for what it was – wrong.

The most unfortunate effect of this life that my parents created for me was the person it did not include. Quietly, patiently, compassionately, my sister had been worked into the background of our family. She learned to participate and encourage the life that had become so routine. She willingly took the blows when the battles came and she made the sacrifices when struggles would arise. Never once did my sister ever complain, never once did she appear jealous or envious. In fact, she almost seemed to thrive in this environment.

I have to come to realize that some people, like

myself, are instilled with the most minimal amount of compassion that takes over when others are hurting, but it is up to us to make the most of what we have been given. Then, I believe that there are those who are blessed with an overabundance of compassion, so much so that they don't even have to work at it, it just comes naturally. I truly believe my sister was one of those naturally compassionate people.

She was there for me in every possible way I needed during that time in my life. There were times when I just needed to be left alone, she would instinctively take control and ensure my much-needed private moments. There were times when I needed a shoulder to cry on and she would lovingly fill that void. When I just needed a gentle ear, she would quietly listen and encourage.

Looking back, I realize without the encouragement, support and love of my whole family, I believe I would not be around today. Whether it would have been from taking my own life, or running away from home or experimenting in drugs, or alcohol in my own attempt to find the comfort and acceptance I desperately wanted from those around me, I feel assured my life would be far from where it is today. But I had a family, who, no matter what I did or how I acted, loved me.

So often in today's society, we see families that are pitifully lacking in the kind of love and support which every child ultimately needs and desires; an unquestionable love that disciplines when they have wronged, comforts when they are sad and rejoices when they have achieved. I never questioned the love my family had for me. Not until many years down the road did I finally realize how special and important our relationship had been, because it grew into a beautiful friendship with each of them, which I now treasure and respect.

The friendship I have with my sister is much more than casual and much more intimate than any friendship I have ever had or probably ever will. Like most sisters, we have seen each other at the best of times and we have seen each other at the worst of times. However, our relationship goes beyond mere observation of circumstances and moves into a deep nurturing and mutual love. It is a relationship that people probably search for most of their lives; one that gives you opportunity and security enough to discuss your most sacred thoughts, one that gives you enough comfort to allow peace in utter silence and one that ignites laughter at the other's expense.

My relationship with my sister is all of that and more and it is that special relationship that helped to illuminate the change that I needed in my own life. It was a such dramatic change, but one I didn't even notice until I was well into adulthood and just starting out with a new life of my own.

I have found that in order to get to that much needed change sometimes we must face and endure some difficult times. And those difficult times often serve as a way for growth. For me, it took watching my sister go through one of the most emotionally traumatic and stressful experiences of her life before I was able to even recognize the embodiment of "self" that had overtaken mine and how far away that position put me from God.

A light didn't go off in my head or I wasn't struck by lightening with this inspiration. I actually just took a casual look back on the previous years and quickly realized that I was no longer even the same person. I was becoming more of what God had always wanted me to be; the person He always knew I could be and the kind of person He wants *all* of His children striving to achieve. He wants us to be caring, giving, sensitive and selfless. These are the attributes I had always admired most in my sister and the ones God would begin to perfect in my life.

CHAPTER 3

As difficult as it is to admit one's mistakes, these same mistakes often serve as a gentle reminder of personal inadequacies and, at the same time, the forgiveness of our Heavenly Father. Of course, we have all made our fair share of mistakes, but there are always a select few, which tend to haunt us and can never be forgotten. We tend to look back on those mistakes with total guilt and shame, but they really should be discerned as God's merciful and loving way of reminding us of the glory He receives as we grow from these mistakes. Because I had yet to allow God to completely take hold of my life, I would continue to make one unforgettable mistake after another. These are not proud moments in my life, but ones I can actually now look back on with humor and a lot of relief; a reminder of a past I feel confident I will never relive.

By the time my sister and I were in high school, we were the best of friends. So, when my sister decided to go off to a small college in Tennessee, it was naturally a very difficult transition for me. Although I thoroughly enjoyed my last two years of high school, I was looking forward to joining her in Tennessee after my graduation.

But God had other plans for me, because it was about the time of my graduation that I began to experience some medical problems.

As a result, I was forced to attend the local college. And it was during this time that both my sister and I met our future husbands. As God had so wonderfully planned it, our future husbands had been best friends since they were young boys. Her boy friend happened to attend a college in Tennessee not far from where she attended and my boyfriend and myself attended the same local college. With my sister's absence and with the establishment of a new relationship, that period of time proved to be the opening of the door to self-discoveries; paving the way for my own transformation, which God had planned just around the corner.

The relationship with my boyfriend was far from what I had always imagined as my "future husband" to be. He was tall, dark and handsome, but he was nothing like the guys I had dated before him. In the 2 years before I met my future husband, I dated a string of guys who gave me everything I ever wanted, but nothing I ever needed. These guys would inundate me with compliments, gifts and praises; giving me the affirmation of self I felt I desperately needed in a relationship. I was dating 4 and 5 guys at a time and relishing in the admiration by all of them. It was exactly what I thought I needed to give me confidence and security in a relationship. Though, when I first began dating my future husband, it was unlike any of my previous experiences.

The relationship immediately started out as a wonderful friendship. He offered to the relationship a terrific sense of humor, a positive outlook on life and a genuinely good character. We thoroughly enjoyed each other's company and spent most every free moment together. But what I soon began to realize was that there was something missing. There were no compliments, there were no gifts and no praises. That just wasn't him. And despite this growing realization, I had become very attached to him. As the weeks turned into months and the newness of the relationship wore off, my insecurities and my need for affirmation reared its ugly head and began to turn our moments together into great scripts for a soap opera.

If it weren't for my future husband's unyielding devotion and his insurmountable patience, our relationship would have been destroyed before it really had a chance to even begin. The fights would always start the same and would always end the same. Girl was feeling insecure. Girl would start fight. Girl would storm out. Girl would come back in tears. Boy would apologize and promise to do better. And girl would be satisfied, for a time. Those kinds of fights would happen so often it became almost comical to the rest of my family.

Despite my attempts to destroy the relationship, he

would never give up on me. He obviously knew the potential our relationship had for something very special and he had made it clear that he wasn't about to let it go. As the months turned into years, the insecurities and, in effect, the fights became less and less. God allowed me to slowly realize I didn't need to reccive affirmation from others to feel good about myself. All I needed was the love of God in my heart and the strength of His powerful shoulders. Just after a year of being together, I knew I was in love with this man God had graciously brought into my life and I knew he was the one I wanted to spend the rest of it with.

When my sister and her boyfriend graduated from college and returned home, the four of us were inseparable. As couples, we each had dated for what seemed like an eternity, making it a running joke among family and friends that the men in our lives planned on remaining in the dating stage for as long as they possibly could. With all the patience and faith we could muster, my sister and I waited for the question we both wanted to be asked.

It was on June 12, 1993 that my sister became engaged. And since my sister's fiancé had been offered a job out of state, they set the wedding date for September 11, 1993. Being only 3 months away, the preparations for it started immediately.

The four of us had been relentlessly teased about doing things together, so everybody suspected my engagement would be just around the corner. And, sure enough, two weeks later, I became engaged. My fiancé and I were still in college at the time and so we set the date for April 30, 1994, after our graduation.

As most of the engaged population is all too familiar with, the closer the wedding day gets, the more chaotic the plans become. Not only for the couple, but also for the families; ordering and addressing the wedding invitations, picking out dress patterns and colors, choosing flowers and decorations and the showers being given. As if that wasn't enough in itself, my mother was also preparing all of the food for the reception and making all of the decorations for my sister's wedding.

So, before we knew it, the preparations had not only overtaken our home with material, flowers, boxes and goodies, but also with lots of work yet to be done. My mother and sister would spend seemingly endless days and nights preparing for the event rapidly approaching. I began to watch them very carefully. I saw the camaraderie they began to share. I saw my mother's pride and joy for my sister. I saw my sister's distracted excitement. All my own excitement and all of my own active involvement in the hustle and bustle of preparing for the big day quickly began to dissipate.

Because it didn't take long before the sight of their developing closeness began to tear away at those feelings of excitement and turning them into feelings of jealousy and envy. Instead of sharing in the thrills of my sister's blessed event, I began to feel irritation at all the attention she was getting; wishing with all my heart that her moment in the sun would quickly be over and I could experience the rewards of my own moment. As ashamed as I am to admit such a hateful part of my personality, I began to withdraw from my relationship with my sister, avoiding her as much as possible.

Whether it was in an attempt to get her upset or keep distance between me and the person who was the source of my jealousy, I don't really know. I really hate to even think it was intentional, but it could have easily been just that. Though, for whatever my true intentions were for my ill behavior, it soon became apparent to both my sister and my mom.

Disappointment was not something my sister and I ever wanted to hear from our mother. She could be upset or angry with us, but when she said she was disappointed with us, it would tear our hearts out. My attitude towards my sister brought out those very words from my mother. Upon reflection, of course, I knew I was being unfair and hurtful towards my sister, but it wasn't until hearing my mother utter those fateful words that made me recognize it for what it was.

I immediately broke down in tears and begged for my sister's forgiveness. In her usual empathetic way, she shared in my tears. We embraced and made up and never spoke of it again.

My wedding took place as we had planned on April

30, 1994. Just before I walked down the aisle, my sister looked at me and smiled. She grabbed my hand and told me how proud she was of me. Tears welled up in her eyes, so I knew my tears were sure to follow. Despite what I had done to her, despite how I had made her feel when she was planning for her own wedding, my sister was nothing but supportive and helpful in preparing for mine. She was my matron of honor, a position I did not want anyone else to have. It was one of the most exciting and thrilling experiences of my life. I was marrying one of my best friends and I had the other at my side to share the moment with me.

CHAPTER 4

My sister and I had always told each other everything; good, bad, hurtful or indifferent. It just wasn't considered fully told until the other had heard the news. That was the way it had always been and we had never known anything different. And being that my sister and I were so incredibly close and we practically did everything together, we decided not to discuss when we would start trying to have children. We were fearful to tell each other would put undue pressure on the other and neither one of us were anxious to create an atmosphere of competition or tension. Since we were so accustomed to running to the other with our news, not sharing such a momentous and exciting decision in our own personal lives was very stressful for the both of us.

Keeping such a decision a secret became almost like a time bomb waiting to explode. We each desperately wanted to know about the other and we each wanted to relay the details about ourselves. I think we both knew it was only a matter of time before one or the other felt compelled enough to break the silence. And true to our beliefs, several months later, we finally revealed to each other the details of our own personal decisions.

I can remember the day vividly. My sister had come to eat lunch with me at the office where I worked. We were all by ourselves. No one else was around; no one else was there to interrupt us. As far I was as I was concerned, I had not planned on revealing anything significant during our time together, but it quickly came apparent to the both of us what a perfect opportunity it was to bring it up.

There was brief moment that was probably not as dramatic as I remember it being, but I can distinctly remember the moment when we both knew what the other was thinking. While we were fixing our lunches, I just happened to glance her way and catch a look that said, "There's something I want to talk about, but I'm not sure I should even bring it up." I returned her slight smile, feeling I knew exactly what she was thinking about. I stopped what I was doing and waited for her to start. In her usual direct way, she blurted out that she wanted the silence about this intimate part of our lives to be over. I wholeheartedly agreed and so, we proceeded to break the ice.

There was actually an initial uncomfortableness I sensed from the both of us, probably from simply fear of the unknown and unexpected. But once we realized what a relief and what a joy it was to be able to share such a significant part of our lives, we both felt kind of silly. A waterfall of emotions and shared experiences quickly began to pour out without any hesitation from either of us.

We soon realized, through our conversation, what an uncanny way God has of bringing such camaraderie and harmony to the most trivial of things. With the close and unique relationship often attributed to twins, my sister and I often experienced moments when our thoughts and feelings seemed as one. And I truly believe that when you spend such a great deal of time together, experiences such as those almost become impossible to avoid. You start acting alike. You start thinking alike. You start talking alike. And after we enlightened each other with our long awaited conversation, we both realized how much this still paralleled our lives. My sister and I found out that we both started trying for children within just a matter of days from each other and we even started earlier than planned for the very same reasons.

Our long awaited conversation lasted for almost 2 hours. During all that time, we shared our many different experiences with trying to conceive. We relayed our own comical stories of our own endeavors to ensure pregnancy and how utterly ridiculous they always seemed afterwards. Though, we also shared some tears, we both came to realize that false hopes become an all too familiar feeling of those who share a desire to bear a child.

Every little physical change, every little emotional change, brought the hopes of the creation of life. As my sister and I found out, it was the disappointments of those false hopes that we also shared. The conversation brought tears, laughter, sorrow and joy, but most importantly, it brought to light our shared experiences, both good and bad, and renewed the joy of our relationship

Several weeks went by without either of us getting pregnant and, as a result, we frequently relied on each other to offer support and encouragement. God knows there will be times of frustration and heartache in His children and knows how important that kind of support and encouragement is to us. And, as such, God called for the establishment of those special kinds of relationships with others.

In Proverbs 17:17, He states, "[a] friend loves at all times, [a]nd a brother is born for adversity". (Sprit Filled Life Bible) This speaks to a kind of relationship that is at its best in times of grief and distress, not only in times of blessing. As close as I am to my husband, it was hard for him to emotionally relate to the frustration and disappointment that often came with each unsuccessful month. So it was such a comfort to be able to have that special kind of relationship with my sister and be able to share those emotions with someone who could relate to them.

Proverbs 17:3 says, "The refining pot is for silver and the furnace for gold, But the Lord tests the hearts". (Sprit Filled Life Bible) Just as heat is used to purify silver and gold, God uses adversity to purify our hearts.

Every one of our unforgettable mistakes, every one of our trials in life, serve to better our hearts; to give us insight, to enable change, to help us grow to be more Christ-like. As difficult as the trials were at the time and as embarrassing as my mistakes were to recall, they would prove to help pave the way for events yet to come in my life.

CHAPTER 5

"Train up a child in the way he should go, [and] when he is old he will not depart from it." Proverbs 22:7 (Spirit Filled Life Bible) This is a scripture my husband and I took very seriously. As a dating couple, we were very open with each other about our wants and desires for children. We were both desirous and excited with the idea of bringing four children into this world. And, before we were even married, we had mutually picked out the names for each one of those 4 children.

We even admitted to each other that we would like to have a little girl first. And we both agreed about how far apart we wanted each of them in ages. But, most importantly, we fervently agreed that bringing a life into this world meant the responsibility of nurturing, loving and guiding those lives in all ways to bring them to a complete commitment and devotion to God. And on October 5, 1995 we would experience the first day in a lifetime of days to mentally and spiritually prepare for that ultimate goal.

That day would prove to be a day of incredible joy for most and searing pain for others. It was a day that I never thought I would see, but one I had been dreaming of before I even got married. October 5, 1995 was the day I found out I was pregnant. The months and months of trying had paid off. The months and months of dreaming had finally come true.

As I am sure most pregnant mothers experience, I could not wait to share the news about my little miracle. And, of course, I wanted my husband to be the first to know. I would often write little notes on the napkin I would place in my husband's lunch. And I had written a poem for my husband several weeks before in anticipation of our first little miracle. So, I transferred my poem to a napkin and convinced my husband to go out to eat.

I took the waitress aside and asked her to give it to him with our meal. He was both thrilled and shocked. After we enjoyed our celebration meal together, we raced over to my parents' home to relay the good news to them. Then we actually tracked down my husband's stepmother at the grocery store where she was shopping. But, the spreading of the news could not stop there. I had to tell my sister. Even though my husband would have preferred to go back home, and even though it was dark outside and most people were settling in for the night, we started traveling to my sister's apartment. As we got closer to her apartment, I thought frantically of the best way to tell her.

A couple of years before, my sister and I had found a pair of little pink infant socks. For some unknown reason, they were the property of my unmarried and childless brother-in-law. At the time, my sister and I were both unmarried ourselves, but we could hear the sounds of the weddings bells and the calls of motherhood quite clearly. So we both wanted to stake our claim to them. We could think of no other way to be fair about the situation except to agree that we would each keep one of the socks and whoever would get pregnant first would be awarded with both socks. I quickly decided that our little sock agreement should be the means I would use to enlighten my sister to my good news.

I filled my husband in on the details of my plans and asked him to just play along with it. As my husband and I casually walked in the door of their apartment, we made some small talk to give the appearance of an innocent and spur of the moment visit. I allowed just enough of the small talk to bait the hook, and then I reeled my sister in and asked, "I just wanted to know, do you still have that pink sock we found, because I want it?" At first, she actually turned to walk in toward her bedroom to apparently go retrieve the sock, and then she stopped in the middle of her stride and turned back around. Her mouth was hanging open and she said, "You mean..." I nodded my head and confirmed what I knew she understood.

True to character, my sister was ecstatic for me. She anxiously inquired about the details. How I found out?

Did I suspect I was pregnant? How far along was I? There is no doubt in my mind that she was genuinely happy for me, but I never really stopped to think about how it would make her feel about *not* being pregnant. We, so often, were able to enjoy the comforts of sharing our own frustrations with each other, it didn't even dawn on me that this might be one more stinging reminder of her own frustrations of still not having conceived.

It was a complete assumption on my part to think that she would be so overwhelmed with my little miracle that her own frustrations would not even be a thought in her own mind. I know she did not have any ill thoughts towards my pregnancy or toward me. But, looking back, I know it must have hurt her. Up until that day, we both had been anxious and frustrated about not being pregnant. We could, at least, share in the camaraderie of those feelings with each other. Now, in one quick moment, I had taken that camaraderie away from her. I could only imagine how painful it was to look at me and realize that I had something that we both had so desperately wanted.

She could not help but be somewhat jealous and pained by the news. I know I would have been if I was in her place. Though, she never let on how much that moment really affected her. In fact, it was not until over a year later that I found out she was forced to seek comfort in her husband's arms after we left their apartment.

Not only did my sister hide the pain she was feeling inside, but she embraced the news of my little miracle with an open and accepting spirit. From the first night she found out, she was nothing but supportive and encouraging. In fact, the first time I saw her after I had told her that I was pregnant, she came bearing gifts. She told me she wanted the baby to receive her very first outfit from her aunt. Although, at that time, I was not aware of the sex of my baby, my sister knew I really wanted a girl. The tiny little outfit almost fit perfectly in my 2 hands. It was pink and white with adorable lacy straps running down the back. The news of my pregnancy hadn't been out a full 2 days and my sister was already the proud aunt wanting to adorn her hopeful niece with gifts.

With the help of my mother, my sister even planned and organized my first baby shower. More than the event itself, she was excited about the gift that she had gotten me for the shower. Even weeks before it, she could talk of nothing but the gift. Without revealing any hints as to its identity, she admitted to me how difficult it was for her to decide what to get and how concerned she was that I would not like it.

When I finally opened her gift, the first thing I saw was a cute little baby dress. A month or so before, I had found out I was having a girl and was anxious to start getting little pink outfits and dresses to clothe my daughter. So, I was thrilled to see the pink flowery dress. When I pulled it out of the box to get a closer look at it though, I realized that there was something else underneath. In the same material that my daughter's dress was made, was an identical dress for me.

My sister had made my daughter and me matching dresses. For a moment, I don't believe I said or did anything. I was so incredibly touched, it was all I could do not to cry. I could not have asked for anything more special. I knew for some, sewing is a very relaxing and enjoyable past time, but knowing my sister the way I do, I know that it is anything but that for her. So, to know that she took the time and effort to do something she does not particularly even like to do, made the gift all the more special. I'm sure the fears and concerns of my approval, the frustration she probably experienced with making the dresses come together and the repressed feelings of pain in her own life played a significant part in that moment.

Because soon I could see the tears of all those mixed emotions pooling in her eyes. I looked over at my mom and realized she was tearing up too. It was a moment, which lasted for just a matter of seconds, but one that touched the hearts of all those present.

CHAPTER 6

Infertility is probably one of the scariest words to couples who desire to bring life into the world, of wanting to pass down their name to someone, and to have someone to nurture, protect and love. For most couples who share this desire, words like infertility would not be on their minds. Although there are an extraordinary number of factors that must happen for conception to actually occur, statistics show that 80% of all couples will be able to conceive within 12 months of unprotected intercourse. Of those who do not conceive even after the full 12 months, only one in seven continue to have problems. So, it may not happen frequently, but infertility is a reality in our society. And to those women who experience it, it can be a devastating and humiliating stigma and a direct insult to the very heart of their womanhood. This was an experience my sister became all too familiar with.

It had been over a year since my sister and her husband started trying to conceive and yet without any success. So, shortly before I had my daughter, my sister and her husband started going to a fertility clinic. The clinic ran numerous tests on both of them and was quickly able to determine the cause of their inability to conceive. The clinic discovered that my sister was not ovulating and, consequently, not able to create the necessary conditions for fertilization. In order to create those conditions, my sister was told that she would have to undergo several time consuming and, at times, difficult series of steps.

Among many other things, it involved taking pills to start the ovulation process, visiting the specialists several times a month to monitor the process and having to plan those intimate moments with her husband to ensure the right timing of it all.

I cannot imagine a more difficult and more distressing way of trying to create life with your spouse. Most dream of a more romantic and passionate setting, not a sterile and fertile environment. It becomes a chore and not something done out of pure pleasure and love for each other. And I'm sure my sister was no different from most in that regard. However, my sister was very encouraged by having a plan and was quite anxious to start the process. But month after month, she would start the process and month after month, it would prove to be unsuccessful. Gradually, I could see the joyful anticipation that she felt only months ago wear away to reveal the first hints of a lot of pain and frustration.

My sister had always been there for me in every way possible. Through all my depression and through all of my sorrow, she had been my encourager, my advisor, my protector, and always, my friend. Now, my sister was facing her own sorrow and the situation would put each of us in very different roles. They were roles neither one of us had really ever experienced before, but they were ones we were destined to fill. I felt ill equipped and unprepared to fill that role. I was at a loss for words and even at a loss of how to act. I so desperately wanted to be there for her, even though I knew that this role for me was practically uncharted territory. I felt totally out of my element.

My own previous sad attempts at being a comfort to others could in no way have prepared me for this. Such a volatile and sensitive subject would require a lot of compassion and warmth, which were characteristics I had never truly felt capable of expressing. How do you comfort in a situation like this? You can't give her what she so desperately wants and you can't patch up her heart like a hole in order to fill the emptiness she feels?

No matter how much praying I did for those very things, I knew that the only way I *could* comfort was just simply to be there for her. So often my sister had been the shoulder I would cry on or the rock I would lean on or the security I would cling to. Now the tables were turned and it was my turn to be all of those things for her and to give just a little bit back of what she had given me for so many years.

Even though I had the best of intentions and my heart was in the right place, the reality of the role I was about to play became very overwhelming. I still felt totally inadequate to be what she needed me to be for her. I knew she needed a comforter, a shoulder and an encourager, and it took everything that was in me to be all those things for her. But it wasn't overwhelming just because it wasn't in my nature to be those things, it was also because those things would prove to be like a double-edged sword.

I felt like if I didn't even ask how she was doing, then she might think that I didn't care. Then I felt if I did ask her, it would just be another painful reminder of what I'm sure she tried so hard to forget. I wanted to be able to do so much more for her than just being that backboard to bounce her emotions off. Though, as difficult as it was for me to be just that, I felt that there was not much else I could do other than pray. Thankfully God never gives you anything He will not equip you to handle, and it was with His strength and endurance that gave me the power to be all of those things for my sister, despite my fears and feelings of failure.

Unfortunately though, it was because I never truly let go of those negative feelings, I opened the door for Satan and allowed him to take advantage of my vulnerability. Satan is always looking for opportunities to break the bonds of our relationship with God and with fellow Christians. Without the confession and repentance of our sins, Satan so easily and so often has those opportunities. Over a period of time, those fears and feelings of failure grew into feelings of guilt. And it was this guilt that would end up dominating much of my life for the next couple of years.

"Survivor's guilt" is a medical term often associated with those persons who are persecuted with thoughts of reproach for the sparing of their lives from some kind of tragic event. In a small way, that was exactly how I started to feel. Without sounding too absurd, I began to feel guilty for my successful conception and the natural joys that usually go along with it. God made the creation of life itself so magical and awe-inspiring. Just the idea naturally draws not only family and friends towards the protruding belly, but complete strangers.

It is just one of those many joys that one expects from being pregnant, to be able to share all of the details and excitement of it with others. It was the easiest thing to accept that attention - as long as my sister was no where around. However, if my sister were sitting near me or around me, despite how much I wanted to thoroughly enjoy the attention, it was hard for me not to cringe inside and feel complete freedom to enjoy them. But for 9 months, it was an endless series of showers, gifts, comments, questions and congratulations and, as a result, I spent the better part of my pregnancy wishing it all away.

As difficult as it had been to go through so many months drenched in guilt, it was nothing compared to the anxiety I was feeling about my daughter's arrival, which was quickly approaching.

I imagined that it would be easier for my sister to ignore the pain when the little life inside me was out of sight, but once there was a face to the life, it would probably be virtually impossible to ignore the pain that she was desperately trying to forget in her own life.

Once my daughter blessed us with her presence and made her way into our lives, I couldn't help but wonder how my sister would face the pain and face the intrusion that was about to come.

No matter how unfounded it may have been, my greatest fear was that jealousy would invade her thoughts and, in affect, begin to deteriorate our relationship. That very fear just goes to prove how easily Satan can take something so precious and use it against us.

My sister had never failed me before and had been nothing but supportive to that point, and yet I was doubting the very nature of who she was and the bond that united us.

CHAPTER 7

As seemingly real and accurate as television can depict bringing life into the world, it can never prepare you for your own personal experience. For first time mothers, like myself at the time, television was usually all you had to rely on as a basis for that event. It was on May 30, 1996 that I would have first hand knowledge of how sad those depictions were and how truly miraculous the experience could be. My water broke at 12:30 a.m. that morning and at 5:30 a.m., we called our families to let them know we were leaving for the hospital.

Thrilled, excited, relieved, anxious, and fearful. There were so many different emotions that played such a vital role in making it one of the most wonderful experiences of my life. And there is no better feeling than to share such an experience with those you love. Unfortunately for some of those loved ones, the rules of the hospital dictated that only 4 people could be in the room during the delivery.

Taking into account all of the soon-to-be grandparents, family and friends, the selection of those 4 people would have ultimately left out several who so wanted to be a part of my daughter's arrival. Although

I hated the thought of leaving anybody out, in my mind, the decision was quite clear. It had been my mom and dad who brought me into this world with all the love and security one could have ever asked for, my sister who had been my constant companion and encourager and my husband who was now my lifelong partner and friend. These were the loved ones I wanted by my side for the arrival of my daughter.

My mom and dad arrived not too much longer after we had gotten settled in my labor and delivery room. They came with cameras and giddy smiles on their faces, very ready for whatever long wait they may have for the birth of their grandchild. My sister was not there yet, but assured me she would be there as soon as she could. She had to stop by and pick up the 2 little boys she babysat, then she would drive straight to the hospital from there. Once she finally arrived, she had to wait for one of the other family members to get there so they could watch the boys and allow her the opportunity to come in the room with me. So, by the time she actually got in the room, she was quite the nervous wreck. She admitted she actually had to stop the car and pray to God for my daughter's safe delivery and her own calm spirits.

Several hours after my family arrived, the contractions got more intense and my daughter's arrival became much more imminent. I pushed for about 15 minutes and watched the faces of my loved ones as the baby began to make her appearance. I pushed for another 5 minutes and then watched their faces light up with joy as my daughter arrived into the world. My mom and sister shrieked with delight as tears streamed down their faces.

The day I had been anxiously waiting 9 months for brought the arrival of our beautiful, healthy baby girl. The experience was better than I could have ever imagined and more amazing than words could even describe. What made it even much more special was the fact that I had the people who meant the most to me there to experience it with me.

CHAPTER 8

Although I was still riding high on the excitement of new motherhood, I knew the fear that had plagued me for months would soon be tested for its reality. I had been home from the hospital for several days, but this was my first Saturday home. I knew that Saturday's events would most likely prove or disprove what I had feared for so long.

Saturdays, for my sister and me, had ritually become the day she and I spent together. Whether it was going to the mall, garage sale hunting or just going out to eat, it was our day to do whatever we wanted. We never really did much planning for those days, it usually started with she or I calling the other around 9:30 a.m. and it was at that time we would discuss the day's events.

I remember this particular Saturday like it was yesterday. My husband and I had our daughter on a schedule that started at 6:30 a.m. in the morning. That schedule afforded us the opportunity to have some quality family time together before my husband had to leave for work. And since my daughter was sleeping much of her day away at that time, once my husband left for work, I had plenty of free time to myself.

Unfortunately for that day, too much time to myself ultimately meant exacerbating my already heightened fears.

The early morning hours dragged by as if it was moving in slow motion. I felt like I could almost hear every minute tick by on the clock. My husband had already left for work, my daughter was asleep, my mom was on her way over to see the baby, but I had yet to receive a call from my sister. Normally, if she had not called by 9:30 a.m., I would call her, but for some reason I could not bring myself to make that call. I was literally watching the dead phone, mentally trying to ring it to life. I was waiting with baited breath for a phone call that, I believed, would seriously affect my life; a phone call that held my fate in its coming.

It may seem so overly dramatic, but these feelings were very real and the moment held a great deal of drama in it for me. The absence of that one phone call all but meant to me the end of a special relationship and friendship I had come to count on over the course of my entire life. I was actually almost to the point of tears when the telephone finally rang. It was her!! If my sister had listened hard enough, she probably could have heard the relief in my voice. After we had talked for a few minutes about how the baby and I were doing, she confessed that she was hesitant about calling because, amazingly, she had her own fears about how this new little life would affect our relationship.

It was almost a comfort to hear that she was having the same kind of fears that I was experiencing. It was this revelation that confirmed my own belief Satan was working hard to destroy something we knew to be so precious. Satan knows if he can destroy the very foundation of family relationships, he is well on his way to destroying the commitment and devotion we have in God. It was very unlike my sister to give in so easily to paranoia and fear. So I knew that this relationship was not only precious in our own eyes, but in God's eyes as well.

The fears and the doubts we both apparently had been plagued with for so long vanished in just a matter of seconds. Satan's best laid plans to destroy our precious relationship only backfired, because I believe it was the reassurance of each other's own fears that helped to strengthen a relationship which might have been torn apart by the secrecy of those unfounded fears.

By the end of the conversation, we were enjoying a good laugh about how silly we had been and we even ended our conversation by discussing our plans for the day's events. Although we only planned to spend the time at my house taking care of the baby and enjoying each others company, it was the mere joy of simplicity and the idea that the "us" was going to be just fine which made that day so memorable.

CHAPTER 9

After 3 months of me crying and whining, my husband still thought it was best for me to go back to work, at least part-time. It was a very difficult decision. There wasn't a night that went by I did not go to bed in tears, dreading the day that I never wanted to see come.

I knew my husband's ultimate desire was for me to be able to stay home with our daughter, but I also knew that he was concerned if his new business would be able to independently support the growing needs of the family. As much as I appreciated those concerns for our financial welfare, I confided in my sister there was a small part of me that was irritated at his decision. There was the small comfort that the babysitter had been a lifelong friend who just happened to live across the street from the place where my mom worked. But it was just that, a small comfort, because it did nothing to ease the dread I felt inside. My sister comforted me, as best she could, and reassured me it would probably be much easier than I expected it to be.

When the day finally arrived, despite the reassurances and prayers of family and friends, I still had prepared myself for a full day of trauma and tears.

Although it was very difficult to think of anything other than the daughter I sorely missed, I made it through the day without much more than a whimper.

It was with a visit from my sister and with those prayers and support of family and friends I know that I made it through and, most importantly, that I could make it through every day if I had to. When I finally left for the day, I found a note on my car that my sister had left for me. She wrote:

> *Leslie –*
>
> *I know how hard this day must have been for you – but I want you to know how proud I am of you for enduring. One day your daughter will be able to share this same pride – in knowing that her mom sacrificed her desires for the benefit of the family. It takes a lot of courage. I love you!*

My sister had such a wonderful gift of knowing exactly what to say and exactly when to say it. As difficult as the day had been, it was those very words from my sister that would allow me to remember that day with fondness. Not only because I made it through the day despite the dread, but also for the realization that I had been blessed by so many supportive family and friends and the reassurance they would always be there for me.

CHAPTER 10

My husband and I felt led to participate in parenting classes that were offered through a couple at our church. We had heard so many good things about these classes and, personally, had seen the impact it could have on the whole family. And so, we spent one night a week for 8 weeks being instructed and taught the biblically based concepts of the classes.

The basic concept of all the classes is to see the child as a welcomed addition to the already established family and not the center of it. All the principles, teachings and instructions in the classes revolved around that one concept. And in keeping with that concept, the classes stressed the importance of putting a baby on a schedule that will suit the entire family. A schedule would put the parents in control and, at the same time, allow the baby to adjust to the schedule the parents had established.

It was a wonderful idea. My daughter adjusted easily to the schedule, making our lives a lot less harried. As much as the schedule helped to produce sanity to our naturally chaotic lives, it was our responsibility, as parents, to maintain that schedule and, ultimately, sacrifice some of our own desires to do just that.

The sacrifices we agreed to make when we established a schedule not only affected us but our extended family. And our extended family not only consisted of my husband's parents and my parents, but also my sister's in-laws as well. My husband spent an immense amount of time as a teenager and a young adult with this family and considered them as much a part of his family as his own. And the feelings were mutual. Spending so much time with that loving and godly family myself over the years, easily brought me to those same feelings. So, in both our minds, the extended family naturally included that family.

It has often been said that there is no greater joy than being a grandparent. You can enjoy all of the thrills of being a parent, spoil them, love them, adorn them with gifts, and then, give them back. And with so many grandparents included in our entire extended family, there were very few occasions when my daughter wasn't at the receiving end of all of their adoration and affection. These grandparents took every available opportunity to indulge themselves in all of the joys of being a grandparent. And being new parents who kept the baby on a schedule, it left fewer opportunities for that indulgence.

Outings with the entire extended family were special occasions. My husband and I were inclined every once and a while to disregard the schedule, but, for the most part, we would make the sacrifices necessary to ensure our daughter's much needed sleep. There were some occasions when the family would invite us out during a time not conducive to our daughter's schedule. And if we felt she could not afford to miss her nap or it was too late for her to be out, then we would decline their invitation. So, when we did go out as a family, it was a major event for everyone.

Being that my daughter was the first grandchild in our family, she, naturally, was the center of attention at these events. She was quite frequently passed from person to person and showered with hugs and kisses. Even my sister and her husband were quite taken with her and were right there with all the grandparents enjoying their own thrills at being an aunt and uncle.

The fears of my daughter being a painful reminder to what my sister so desperately wanted for her own, were no longer a real concern. My sister loved and treated my daughter as if she were her own. I know there were times when she looked at her with a natural want and desire for one of her own, but she more often than not, took her role as an aunt very seriously and delighted in it. My daughter had brought so much joy to the entire family. She was a happy and content little baby who had obviously touched our entire family with her arrival into our lives. It was this attentiveness and regard for my daughter, which eventually uprooted those old feelings of guilt I experienced when I was pregnant. And that same attentiveness and regard, I believe, brought on new fears for my sister.

My sister and I have always shared a special relationship with our mother. We both considered her a friend and someone with whom we thoroughly enjoyed spending time. So, when my sister confessed to me one day that she thought that our mom and I were getting closer because we now shared the bond of parenthood, it was like being hit with a bat. Those were the last words I wanted to hear from my sister. I had struggled so much to keep the feelings of guilt away from my mind. And hearing my sister's confession brought them all right back.

As a teenager, I experienced first hand knowledge of what it was like to be in a relationship involving 3 people. As much as I loved those 2 other friends, sometimes it felt like a constant competition; wondering if they were talking about me, if they were spending more time together or if they appeared to have more in common. It sometimes drove us apart and caused disharmony between all 3 of us. I knew the relationship that I had with my sister and mother was on a much more mature level, but obviously, the same basic feelings and fears were still present.

And I'm sure my sister's fears were only exacerbated by the amount of time that our mother was spending with my daughter. She was a typical doting grandmother, wanting to spend most free moments wrapping her arms around the new little life. Although my sister never spoke of those fears again, I believed my assurances to her, that parenthood could not change the love and relationship our mother had with each of us, failed to ease her mind.

The fear my sister was experiencing concerning our mother was also coupled with similar fears concerning her in-laws. Although she never shared those particular fears with me, I can only imagine how painful it must have been for my sister to see the love they had for my daughter as well. They seemed to take to my daughter just as I would expect them to take to their own grandchild. I know my sister must have desperately ached to be able to give them a grandchild of their own and give them their own thrills of grandparenting. And I know they probably ached just as much to have their own grandchild.

So, at times, it was really difficult for me to even watch her in-laws show any kind of attention at all to my daughter; attention I wanted them to be able to show to my sister's own child.

The months quickly passed by and our family watched my daughter grow and change right before our very eyes. With each new development came the excitement and pride shared by the whole family. We all enjoyed the little life God had added to our family all the while praying my sister would be blessed with an addition of her own. My sister experienced the same excitement and pride in her niece, while, at the same time, consistently praying for a child of her own, which would restore the confidence and dignity often lost with infertility.

CHAPTER 11

As often as my sister had to go to the doctor and as ritualistic as the process had become, I was usually well aware of my sister's month to month routine. I knew she would be going to the doctor's office soon to check the results of the fertility procedures for that particular month. I didn't know, though, what particular day it would be. After several months of unsuccess, I had come to learn not to inquire into the details of the results quite as often.

I still tried to maintain the open relationship with her, allowing her the freedom to express her frustrations and sorrow every now and then, but I quickly realized an inquiry after each unsuccessful month sometimes added to her frustration. Her thoughts became like a book to me. I would back off when I sensed the frustration, tried to encourage when I sensed the sorrow and would offer a willing ear when I sensed her need for release. Being frustrated myself and discouraged by my sister's situation, I had come to almost expect another unsuccessful month and was already preparing myself to try and sense what she needed from me for yet another disappointment.

Driving home from work, it never even crossed my mind that this would be the month that might turn out very differently than I expected. As I was getting closer to my babysitter's house located at the far end of the street, I thought I saw my sister's car. Then, out of the corner of my eye, I recognized my sister standing on the sidewalk like she was waiting for someone. I just assumed she was about to visit our mom who worked across the street, but when she saw my car, she headed straight for me.

As I slowed down the car to pull along side the street, I eased by my sister and gave her a casual smile. Just as I was about to turn my head, I saw her mouth these words to me; "I'm pregnant". With the shock of the unexpected good news, I tried vainly to push on the brake, put the car in neutral, get off my seatbelt and open the car door, all at exactly the same moment. It was only by the grace of God that I brought my car to a complete stop and was able to get myself safely out of it. This was the news our family and friends had been praying about for months. We shared in her frustration, we shared in her sorrow and now we were going to be able to share in her joy. I was ecstatic. We ran to each other, threw our arms around each other and cried like babies.

I have been known to posses quite a flare for the dramatic. Since I had to act my way through much of my teenage life, it was a talent I perfected over the years and one I enjoyed dappling in whenever I could. My sister, on the other hand, you could read like a book. A poker player she could never be. The good news my sister had to share with the rest of the family was too important not to indulge in a little of the dramatic. And, being that I was the very first one to find out, I felt it was my responsibility and privilege to create the scene for the unveiling of her news.

I threw out ideas left and right, I enlightened her with my suggestions and even offered her my acting services, but in the end, she sweetly rejected them all. Instead, I convinced her to allow me, at least, the privilege of being there when she told our mom and dad. Once she agreed, I asked for one more favor. I told her I would allow her the opportunity to tell her husband in private, if only she would tape record his reaction. Throughout all of the testing, throughout all of the heartache, her husband had never really said a word. And as quiet as her husband had been about their difficulties in conceiving, I knew he ached for a child just as much as my sister did. I knew his reaction would be priceless.

I was able to easily lay the groundwork for me being present when our parents were told of the good news, since my husband and I had already planned to visit them later that evening. We had to drop something by their house, so I told my sister to drop by around 7:30 p.m. and we would already be there visiting. I told her to act like they just decided to visit and we would act surprised to see them. As I saw the front door opening, I innocently inquired of my mom, "Are you expecting anyone?" as I pointed to the opening door.

She looked puzzled, and then she saw the faces through the front window. My mom opened the door for them with delighted surprise. We made small talk for a few minutes and then my sister and her husband followed my mom into the kitchen and casually said, "Do y'all really want to be grandparents?" Of course with both her and her husband wearing goofy grins from ear to ear, my mom and dad knew exactly what that meant.

It was not the dramatic performance that I would have made it to be, but the look on my mom's face was beyond words and was worth it all. It's very difficult for parents to see their children hurting and I knew, if it would have helped my sister conceive my mother would have torn off her right arm. My mother immediately started crying and the rest of us soon followed.

It had been such a long time since I saw my sister so content and happy. Like most soon-to-be-mothers, she immediately wanted to share the good news with loved ones and wanted to start making plans for the upcoming event. Because so many people were aware of the difficulties she and her husband had in conceiving, it wasn't long before they were being inundated with presents and congratulations.

Despite my elation for my sister's long awaited

pregnancy, I confessed to my husband one day that I was a little bit jealous of my sister. It was no more than just a passing feeling and it no way resembled the jealousy I experienced when I was younger. There were no thoughts of wishing it were me in her place and wishing to take any of the attention away from her. My sister had been through so much sorrow and pain up to that point, I relished in the life God had blessed her with and would never dream of taking away any of the joy and attention she was now able to experience.

My statement was more a statement of regret than jealousy. I had wished most of my pregnancy away and continued to struggle with feelings of guilt for even months after. And now watching my sister experience the excitement of being pregnant, the wonders of the miracle and the attention that it drew, I was wishing it all back. It would only be a matter of days later when the mere thought of that passing feeling would bring regret of its own.

The following Saturday started out no different than any other Saturday for my sister and me. That morning we had talked and planned to visit every baby store and garage sale in the area searching for all the necessities for her upcoming event. My sister even managed to leave earlier than planned to venture out on her own and that's just a virtual struggle for her in itself. We were all excited and my daughter and I were ready to go when my sister pulled up in front of the house. But as she started to get out of her car, I immediately noticed something was terribly wrong.

Although she refused to even look at me as she approached the open door, her very demeanor screamed in anguish. As she passed by me, it was obvious she had been crying and I asked her what was the matter. She looked up at me with tears streaming down her face and said, "I'm bleeding!"

I didn't want my sister to know exactly what I was thinking, but everything I had ever heard told me this is not welcomed news. I told her not to worry about anything until we had something to worry about. She talked to her doctor and they made an appointment for later that day. The doctor advised her to relax and keep her feet up.

So we canceled our plans for that day and decided just to stay in together. I knew she must have been feeling such dread, worrying about the unknown or the unspoken. I certainly didn't want her to dwell on the subject and it was obvious she just wanted to put it out of her mind as much as possible. What could be said? What could be done? Our plans had abruptly come to a halt in the wake of a possible tragedy. Although we made no further mention of the conversation with the doctor or spoke nothing of the baby, I knew it was foremost in our thoughts.

I wanted her to be able to forget the feelings of dread, at least, for the moment, and comic relief might be the only way for that to happen. So, I picked out a comedy that I was sure would make her laugh. I knew the movie would only postpone the doubts that were sure to return, but for that moment, the anguished look had left her face and allowed her to forget for a while.

The next day I got a call from my sister. The anguished face I had seen yesterday had returned in the voice at the other end of the phone. All she said was "I lost the baby!" She was obviously crying and I knew she wouldn't want to talk on the phone about it right now. So, I told her how sorry I was and we both just hung up.

"In this you greatly rejoice, though now for a little while, if need be, you have been grieved by various trials, that the genuineness of your faith being much more precious than gold that perishes, though it is tested by fire, may be found to praise, honor and glory at the revelation of Jesus Christ." 1 Peter 1:5-7 (Spirit Filled Life Bible). As Christians, it is quite often beyond our understanding of what God's purpose is for such a seemingly senseless loss. And as Christians, we are not to question the reasons for these kinds of tragedies, but to faithfully trust in His perfect will for each of us.

But as natural sinners, that unquestionable faith is one of the most difficult tasks before us; to look at death, tragedy and tribulation straight in the face and smile, knowing that God's glory will be found through it. My sister's phone call had left me immediately feeling a sense of regret. The innocent statement I made not just a couple of days ago expressing some amount of jealousy toward my sister was coming back to haunt me. The irrational and ridiculous invaded my mind. "Is God punishing my sister for my jealousy?" "Am I somehow responsible for her loss?" They were horrific thoughts I hated to even admit to myself, much less to others.

I kept those feelings and thoughts to myself, afraid and ashamed to even speak the words aloud. Thankfully, though, my husband actually sensed the beating I was giving myself and brought sanity and sobriety to my irrational emotions. He reminded me that our God is not a God of vengeance and retribution, He is a God of compassion and mercy. And that the loss should in no way put blame on anyone, but just accepted as being a part of God's plans.

To grieve is human. It's a necessary part of healing, without which the closure to the tragedy would never come full circle. And even though this was a tragedy like none other my sister had ever experienced, I felt assured that she would struggle her way through the grieving process in no time at all.

Since I had always come to see my sister as being an indestructible pillar throughout her life and as being a huge source of strength for most of my own life, I hadn't considered anything differently. I couldn't consider anything differently.

But it was quite different. Even several months after the subsequent loss of her baby, it was apparent the tragedy still weighed heavy on my sister's mind. You could visibly see the despair and pain in her eyes. The giddy joy and carefree attitude that characterized much of our lives was gone. She was even reluctant to talk, and when she finally did, she revealed a depressed side of her I had never seen before. It was a side I thought I would *never* see in my sister and one I never wanted to see again.

Through tear-filled eyes, my sister confessed to me there was not a day that went by when she didn't think about the baby. She continued by telling me she was tired of all the tests and rituals she had to go through every month and the frustrations and anxieties, which accompanied them. The statement that scared me the most, though, was when she said she would rather be dead than to continue to go through this month after month. She said that not being able to have a child was as close to Hell as she would ever see.

As much as my sister's words frightened me, it was more frightening to realize that the person I looked up to, my constant source of strength and encouragement, was now in desperate need of those very resources that she was always giving to me. She needed a supporter, an encourager.

This was a role I felt compelled to fill, but one I still felt God was continuing to perfect in my life. Once again, I found myself asking, "How do I even go about being the supporter and encourager she is in desperate need of right now?" In just a few short days, my sister had grown to love and cherish the very life developing inside her. And now, in the blink of an eye, the life was gone. It may have been a short life, but it was a life she quickly embraced and one that opened up a whole new world for her. It gave her new hope and new joys like she had never experienced before.

Everything my sister dreamed of with this new life was ripped right from her grasp. There was no warning for her, no time for her to say goodbye. She was understandably devastated. I knew that the experience would be something she would never forget and that it would always be a part of her somehow. With God at my side and a determination in my heart, I was prepared to help make sure the experience would be remembered as bringing glory to His name.

My sister expressed her fears that she would someday forget about the baby. And as difficult as I knew that would be for her to do, I wanted to address those fears and do something that would carry on the baby's memory forever. There was always a certain amount of temerity and lack of self-confidence on my part, but I felt assured of God's direction in my life and knew God had empowered me with an ability and creativity I never knew was in me. And with this empowerment, I knew exactly what I wanted to do for my sister.

Gideon's International is a world-renowned

organization, which distributes Bibles to places all over the world. I understood that they also accepted dedications, in part, as a donation to help continue their ministry. In memory of my sister's baby, I dedicated 2 of those Bibles and along with the Certificate of Dedication for the Bibles, I wrote my sister this poem:

> *Though your baby's life*
> *On this earth he never saw,*
> *He had already touched and affected*
> *Ours one and all.*
> *Though his young life*
> *Will remain with us forever,*
> *This gift will assure it*
> *To touch others wherever.*

My sister's appreciation and emotions alone were enough to make that moment very special, but it was also my own realization of what God had done for me and where He had brought me. Up to that point, I couldn't even recall an occasion that I had ever made more than a passing effort for someone else. Sure, I had given gifts, sent cards, listened and tried to encourage. But I don't recall ever putting so much thought into something for someone else, for no other reason than to give of myself for someone else's sake. There was no personal desire, no personal gain or selfish motive involved. It was purely a selfless act. This realization was in no way just to pat myself on the back; it was the thrill that God had given me a special gift and the ability to use that gift to bring glory to His name.

CHAPTER 12

It had been a year since my daughter arrived into our lives. The elaborate celebration was planned, which would, no doubt, be filled with lots of presents and doting family and friends. As excited as I was about sharing such a significant milestone with all the people I loved and cherished, I couldn't help but wonder how difficult the celebration would be for my sister. She had just recently experienced the loss of her own child, now she would be celebrating the life of another's child. I wondered if watching all of the attention and adoration from her own family and friends would be too much of a reminder of a little life she sorely missed.

The celebration was quite extravagant for just a one year old little girl. We had balloons, cake, ice cream, banners and presents galore. When all the guests arrived on that day, we had about 20 adults. It looked like a media conference one would expect for a famous Hollywood movie star. There were probably 6 different cameras all flashing at different times and then there was a video camera going to record every special moment. As happy and content as I was at the time, I would often glance her way to make sure there were no visible signs of any pains of the past.

If that day had pained my sister in any way, it was neither evident by her face nor the thoughtfulness that she brought with her. In addition to the gift that my sister and her husband bought for my daughter's birthday, she also gave me a book that she had written for my daughter. It was a children's book about things that parents may not vocally or mentally wish for their children, but things that happen in today's harsh and cruel world that may, ultimately, help to encourage them to be godly examples.

It was a beautiful and wonderfully written book. I was touched not only by my sister's thoughtfulness but more importantly, by the incredible amount of love and adoration she exhibits towards my daughter. Childless and pained by that realization, she is still able to find every opportunity to give of herself to demonstrate the special bond she feels for my child and, ultimately, to show the strength of character that God gives to His children.

Ever since I could remember my sister has had a gift with words. She had written short stories, poems, and essays. It was apparent from the beginning this was the gift with which God had blessed her. And on numerous occasions, our family had tried to encourage her to publish some of the things she had written. Though, as talented and wonderful as I believe my sister was, she lacked the aggressiveness and desire to make that a reality. With the book she had written for my daughter in my possession, I thought there would be no better way to say "thank you" than by trying to get it published.

After months and months of my own editing and revising, I sent a copy of the finished product to a friend of mine who was willing to illustrate the book for me. Along with his copy of the book, I had written a description of the scenes I wanted associated with each page of the book so he knew exactly what I wanted him to draw. Once he had completed the drawings, I wanted to get it copyrighted and published, then present it to my sister as a gift.

CHAPTER 13

"I waited patiently for the Lord; and He inclined to me, and heard my cry. He also brought me up out of a horrible pit, out of the miry clay, and set my feet upon a rock, and established my steps. He has put a new song in my mouth – Praise to our God; many will see it and fear, and will trust in the Lord." Psalm 40 (Spirit Filled Life Bible). The apostle Paul poetically describes in these verses how out of the tragedies of life, God lifts us up and gives us renewed strength. This is something He has promised us as Christians, to bring His glory out of our tragedy. My sister had experienced her own tragedy and now God was preparing her heart for His glory.

It had been several months since my sister lost her baby. She had been sitting at the bottom of the pit for longer than I cared to remember. She even had me worried enough to question whether I would ever see her come out of it. But, with God's compassionate, healing hands, she did come out of it. She was finally able to give all the heartache of her loss into God's hands, trusting in His promise to us as Christians. And, although it took much longer than I expected it to, God, in His perfect timing, rewarded her faithfulness and allowed the wounds and sorrow to heal.

It was an amazing and inspiring transformation. My sister began to visibly pull herself out of that pit. I began to see her struggle to regain her confidence as well as her identity. The vibrant, fun-loving woman who we all knew, respected and loved was returning with a renewed perspective on life. A perspective, which I knew, could have only come from God. As many people who were praying that my sister would be blessed with a child were also praying that the heartache and trauma of these events would be replaced with peace. My sister had found that peace through God and proved again, the power of prayer!

As for many of us, it is difficult not to sometimes wander back from where God had brought us. And my sister was no different. The peace she had found was still there. The renewed perspective she had gained was still there. My sister had won the war. But, naturally, the daily battles in the war of life would sometimes take their toll on her and cause her to crumble to her knees in tears. It was her little way of remembering, allowing herself the freedom to experience all of the emotions with it, while finding comfort in God's arms.

CHAPTER 14

In mid December, my husband and brother-in-law convinced my sister and me to venture off to Myrtle Beach for a 3-day vacation. They were anxious to get their fill of golf and enticed my sister and me with thoughts of having no wifely or motherly duties to dominate much of our day. It wasn't a hard sell so my husband and I arranged for our daughter to stay with my mother-in-law, then the four of us took off to live the next 3 days worry free.

While the guys were getting up at the crack of dawn to play golf in the freezing cold weather, my sister and I slept late, rented movies, read books and basically lived the bum's life until the guys came back in the afternoon. Then we would go out to dinner at a nice restaurant, would tour the area and come back to enjoy a cup of my famous hot chocolate. We had a great time.

On the very last day there, my sister and I had to wait for the guys to finish their last round of golf. We probably waited for about an hour and it was during that time my sister and I engaged in a conversation, which made the weekend all the more memorable.

The conversation was far from being planned but

seemed to naturally work its way in. I am not really quite sure what triggered the conversation. But, I believe we started talking about my daughter. My sister expressed to me how much she and her husband completely adored her and how proud she was of me as a parent. I asked her to tell me how things were progressing at the fertility clinic. And she explained to me that she and her husband were taking a break. The months and months became too stressful and they mutually decided it was best to stop for a while at least. My sister proceeded to tell me that she had been doing a lot of thinking about the possibility of me having another child soon. She said she really believed that she could handle that possibility and in fact, would welcome such a joyous occasion, if the next baby were anything like my first child.

I never once thought my sister meant that statement to sound selfish or proud, as though she was giving me permission to have another child. If it had been anybody else, maybe I would have misconstrued the meaning. But I knew my sister's loving and compassionate heart. In her own way, she was saying not to let her own personal difficulties cause any anxiety or guilt in me about trying to have another child. It was not something she had to say, but maybe sensing or realizing the guilt I might have been experiencing, she felt the need to ease my mind.

So moved by her statement, I felt the need to express

a few of my own. For months, I have wanted to say something to her, but could never seem to find the perfect moment. That moment couldn't have been any more perfect. So I told her she was such an inspiration to me. I saw in her such a strength and endurance I greatly admired. As with most of Christians, I knew my sister was probably very critical of the way she had handled herself through her situation. And I assured her God doesn't expect perfection, he expects faith, patience, and endurance; characteristics which she displayed throughout it all.

She told me she had never been bitter towards God. Despite the emotional and even physical drain the experience brought to her, she held tightly to her faith and hope. She went on to say she actually would never want to change what she had gone through. She could see so much good out of it, she knew it was all from God. She was stronger physically, emotionally and spiritually. She also said in her heart of hearts, believed that God would bless her with a child and that God was just teaching her continued patience and faith. Here I was looking at a woman who was going through something I could never even begin to imagine and she was an encouragement to me.

If this godly woman was not a true example of God's awesome power and wisdom, I had no idea what would be. By the end of our conversation, we were both blubbering idiots. We were in the midst of an embrace and retelling each other how much we loved the other when we spotted our husbands on the last hole. I cannot tell you how much of a relief that conversation was to me and I'm sure, for her. It was a conversation that we would probably never speak of again, but a welcome one that we would probably never forget.

CHAPTER 15

My sister and I were exactly 2 years and one week apart in age. And I think our relatively close age difference as young children helped to mold the special bond my sister and I now share as adults. Since I had always wanted to give my own children every opportunity to establish the same special bond among themselves, my husband and I agreed that we would like our children around the same distance apart. My daughter would be turning 2 years old in about 7 months, so we decided it would be a good time to start trying again for another child.

As excited as we were about our decision to try and bring another life into the world, my husband and I kept the effort to ourselves. There was, admittedly, a small part of me, which felt a little bit selfish for even wanting to try for another child when I knew my sister was struggling to have her first. And despite the conversation in Myrtle Beach with her, I wanted to at least be sensitive enough not to put any more pressure and stress on my sister than I'm sure she was already experiencing naturally. In light of the conversation, though, I knew my sister would really want me to go on with my life and my desires to expand our family. I just wasn't ready to make it public.

The feelings of the past all came rushing right back to me. My husband and I made a decision to add to our family, to try and create for our daughter a little sister, to bring a new life into our world, but I couldn't share the frustrations and excitement of it with my sister. I wanted to confide in my sister and I knew she would probably want me to, but it wasn't something I was ready to do. I could confide in my husband to a certain extent, but it was still hard for him to emotionally relate with the frustration and all of the other emotions that go along with it. He was as comforting and sympathetic as one could be who didn't truly understand. But, he did always have a consistently faithful heart, reassuring me of God's perfect plan and perfect timing.

It came at a time when we least expected it, but eventually my husband and I were sharing in the joy of another life given to us by God. We had discussed whether or not we wanted to tell anybody about our news. And knowing I didn't want my sister to know quite yet, we realized we couldn't let a great deal of people in on our new little miracle. We decided that we would only tell my mom and his mom. The rest of family and friends would have to wait until I was ready.

With all of my good intentions, circumstances prevented it from being kept a secret for too long. One night while I was fixing dinner, I started experiencing a little bit of cramping. I didn't think too much about it at the time. Though, just as I sat down with my family to enjoy the meal I prepared, I began to bleed. I was terrified and my face must have shown it, because my husband immediately asked me what was wrong. I ran into the bathroom to confirm my suspicions. By the time I got to the bathroom, the bleeding had basically stopped, but all my thoughts and fears were lingering on the worst.

I immediately called my mother and asked her if she could baby-sit for me the next day so I could go see my obstetrician. He told me to come in first thing in the morning so he could do an examination. When I arrived, I probably only waited a total of an hour for the doctor to see me on such short notice, but the wait seemed like an eternity. God had done so many things for me and had brought me so far from where I used to be. I was no longer the same person and I had no desire to disappoint God or myself and fall so easily back into a world of faithless insecurity.

I had seen my sister go through her own tragedy with strength, endurance and dignity. I wasn't about to let the lesson my sister helped to teach me go to waste. I wanted to show God I had faith in Him and I knew He was going to pull me through this thing no matter what the outcome. My life was in His loving hands and I felt ready for whatever He was about to deal me.

When the doctor finally did come in to examine me,

I was prepared for the worst, but determined to be strong in the wake of the expected news of a tragedy. After a cursory exam and an ultrasound, the doctor asked me if I wanted to look at the results. My only response was, "Should I?" The very sweet, Christian doctor looked at me with his endearing smile and said, "Everything is just fine." I let out a sigh of relief and he went on to say that apparently my body prepared to have twins, but that one of the sacks was collapsing, which was the cause for the cramping and bleeding.

Although I thanked God for the healthy baby, I couldn't help but wonder about the baby that was missing from the second sack. Tears of relief and sadness rolled down my face as my eyes froze on the picture before me; a picture that displayed the plans that God had in mind for me. The doctor could not be sure the empty sack actually held anything other than fluid, but there was the assurance that the other contained a thriving little life that I already loved and would soon be able to hold.

Despite the relief that I felt, I was overcome with emotion and felt somewhat overwhelmed by the events of the last 24 hours. Feeling physically and emotionally drained, my thoughts were not really even on the good news I could share with my mom, but more on the thoughts of going home to the comfort and safety of its walls. I was advised by the doctor to stay off my feet for 2 weeks and I was looking forward to walking through the door and doing just that.

Though to my surprise, when I walked through the door, my sister was standing right there in front of me. My mouth dropped open and I was speechless. My sister assumed that I was at work and asked me what I was doing home so early. I wasn't mentally prepared for a performance in order to keep her unaware of my condition. I knew, though, if I even opened my mouth to say anything at all, it would just be a prelude to an emotional outburst.

As my mom walked into the room, I gave her a look as if to say, "What do I do?" I knew in my heart that the façade was over and that in just a matter of a few moments the truth would be revealed, so I gave in to the emotions that had wanted to surface when I walked through the door. I dropped my head into my hands and cried. My sister's face immediately turned to concern and quickly turned to fear when nobody was saying anything. Once I regained control, I began to tell her the whole story from the beginning to the end; when I found out I was pregnant, when I told our mom, when I started bleeding and the results of the doctor's visit.

Just as I knew she would be, she was more sympathetic than she was hurt. My sister told me she was sorry about the baby I may have lost but was happy that the other baby was just fine. If the news of my second little miracle bothered her, she gave no indication of anything but elation.

I stayed in bed for 2 weeks just as the doctor suggested and it was during that time that another of God's little miracles took place.

CHAPTER 16

It was during a telephone conversation with one of my friends that I first had some inkling of the little miracle that God was about to reveal to our family. It just started with little thoughts at first, but then the thoughts turned into something I could not get out of my head.

I was asked to be in a wedding during the summer and after I found out I was pregnant, I realized that I would be about 7 months along when the wedding finally took place. I thought it was only polite to call my friend and let her know about my expanding condition and to give her the option of whether or not she still wanted to have me in the wedding.

After I explained my current situation to my friend and she insisted I still take part in her wedding, we began to talk in general about the pregnancy and everything that had gone on since I found out. In the midst of the conversation, a thought began running through my head, which I felt compelled to share with my friend. My sister was also going to be in the wedding and for some reason, I felt like I needed to inform my friend my sister was in the exact same condition. I didn't say anything of course, because I had nothing on which to base my idea. In fact, I had no idea why this thought was running around in my head, so I just shrugged it off to wishful thinking and was glad I kept my mouth shut. Little did I know that in less than 24 hours I would find that those very thoughts I had shrugged off would become a reality.

If I had thought hard enough about those "little voices," I would have realized the enlightenment that God was allowing me to enjoy. But unfortunately, I have a reputation for being quite hardheaded. So, it was very much in character for me to require more than just those "little voices" to convince me of its reality. As much as God had done to make it clear to me, I still could not bring myself to even relay the thoughts I was having for fear of it being just wishful thinking of my own. Thankfully, God continued to persist, and eventually I made it my own little mission to test the reality of those "little voices."

This little mission of mine involved getting my sister to somehow prove the truth of those "little voices" without letting her know why I wanted her to do it. This is probably not how God planned on me using the insight He had given me and would have probably preferred a leap of faith on my part, but I just couldn't bring myself to make the leap. Instead, I devised a plan, which I was sure my sister would accept without a second thought.

I had bought a pregnancy test that contained 2 tests. After I had confirmed my own pregnancy several weeks before, I had one test that I would not need for quite some time. I tore off the wrapper on the second test to conceal all the details about the test. And I casually called my sister to tell her I had an extra pregnancy test, which I obviously would not need for some time. I told her it was about to expire and I didn't want it to go to waste. I told her she could take it home with her when she came by later that day. One of my sister's many adoring traits is that she believes everything she is told. Without even questioning, my sister accepted the test and agreed to use it.

Not too long after I convinced her to take the test, I received a call from my sister with an encouraging question. Since I had taken the wrapper off the pregnancy test to conceal the fact that the date was far from being expired, she was left with no instructions on how to read the test. I told her that 2 lines were supposed to appear if you were pregnant. She said that the second line was visible but very, very faint. I couldn't help but get a little over anxious, because I knew that the second line should not appear at all if you weren't pregnant.

Despite my orders to stay in bed, I convinced my mother to let me go to my sister's house since she lived literally only a minute away. My mother reluctantly agreed and so I immediately drove to my sister's house to see if I could give her a more confident opinion. Unfortunately, the line *was* very faint. I could understand her apprehension in even thinking that it might be positive, so I told her it might be best just to go ahead and take another test.

The next day, I received a call from my sister that all of our family and friends had been praying about for 3 years. She said, "I'm pregnant". Though, the news alone was a miracle in itself, it was far from the most miraculous part about those long awaited words. Like my sister had informed me not too long ago, she and her husband had stopped going to the fertility clinic. They mutually decided to take a break. Several weeks after their decision, her husband confided in her that he prayed she would conceive during their break so they could give all the glory to God. That was God's plans from the very beginning. In His perfect timing and in His perfect way.

My sister made an appointment at the fertility clinic the next day. She was expecting only to be a few weeks pregnant, but to everyone's amazement, she was actually nine weeks along, putting her 2 weeks ahead of me. All the frustration, sorrow and pain my sister felt over the past 3 years, was wiped from her mind in a matter of seconds. There was now the excitement and joy she could feel at the thought of God's miracle and blessing; the miracle of life and the blessing of His promises to us. God had promised His glory out of our adversity and in light of her faith and patience, He delivered it to my sister in the little life she now carried.

CHAPTER 17

Before my sister and I were even married, we used to talk about how exciting it would be to be pregnant together. To be able to share our aches and pains, the joys and sorrows, but most importantly, to share in the pleasures and blessings of motherhood. Now, after several years of marriage, after our own personal struggles and after hours and hours on our knees in prayer, God had answered and given us the opportunity to share that very experience together.

Despite how perfect God had planned our situation, my sister and I found it very difficult to not be a little apprehensive because of our previous circumstances. So in dreaming about the future, we just took joy in the day by day moment. Thank goodness our God is merciful and forgiving, because we let Him down more times than we can even count. When the days had turned into weeks and the weeks had turned into months, the apprehension dissipated and we each began to delight in a future with the little miracles God had graciously given us.

When my sister experienced the loss of her first child, all of her family and friends were disappointed because we couldn't even imagine a more perfect time for her to conceive. We prayed with frustration and doubt at such a seemingly senseless loss of life, which brought such despair of heart. What was God doing? And why was He doing it? We would all pray; with little comprehension, but God in His awesome and powerful way, *could* imagine a more perfect time and a more perfect way for my sister to conceive. What didn't make sense to us, brought to light gifts and abilities of my own. Out of the tragedy and despair my sister suffered came understanding, peace and a renewed commitment. God did have a more perfect plan and His glory was revealed in that plan. Yet He still had not unfolded to our family the fullness of His perfect plan and all it would entail.

CHAPTER 18

Just as much as I wanted another daughter, my sister wanted a boy. And everybody, from the very beginning of her pregnancy, thought she was having a boy. I was carrying my baby much the same way I had carried my first daughter. I was carrying higher. I was still very small and barely showing. My sister was carrying very differently from me. She started protruding a little earlier on and she was carrying really low. All of our family and friends felt very assured right up until the very end that my sister was going to be blessed with a boy. I found out when I was about 5 months pregnant that I was going to have another little girl.

My sister, on several different occasions, made attempts to find out what she was having, but was unable to tell from any of the ultrasounds. Although she was perfectly satisfied with not knowing, it became quite frustrating for the rest of the family who desperately wanted the stubborn child to indulge our curiosity. The baby would never cooperate in that area, so we all reluctantly accepted the fact that we would have to be surprised.

On August 19, 1998, my sister had her last doctor's appointment before her due date on August 25. Her previous appointment revealed that the baby was breach, so we were all anxious to hear about the baby's position. After her appointment, she came over to my house to apprize me of any new developments. She said the baby was still breach and the doctor recommended that she schedule a C-section for early next week. I could tell it bothered my sister a little.

She had been so enjoying just being pregnant; it didn't even dawn on her that she might not have a normal delivery. As best I could, I tried to reassure her that not having to go through labor and delivery might be a blessing in disguise. It had been a running joke between my sister and me that the only kind of pain she could handle was the pain of rejection. So I jokingly told her that she probably couldn't have handled the extreme pain that would ultimately come with labor and delivery.

I also told her that even though I would never change the fact that we knew we were having a girl, I sort of envied the extra excitement she was surely going to experience from not knowing. And that in itself would be all worth it. The excitement of the birth alone was much anticipated and then to wait with baited breath to hear the doctor say, "You've got a little baby _____?" My sister easily worked through her anxieties and fears and was anxiously awaiting the birth of her child scheduled on August 25, 1998.

On August 25, 1998, the waiting room was filled

with family and close friends. Every so often one of us would peek out the door to see if we could see the new arrival coming down the hall! It was 2 hours later when one of those trips out the door revealed my mother skipping anxiously down the hall with the most mischievous grin spread across her face. She silently stood there in front of the waiting room doorway as if she had nothing to say to us. I finally said, "Well?" She simply replied, "I'll let him tell you!"

The waiting room had emptied and we had all piled outside the door waiting for the new father and the rest of his entourage to come down the hall. What only took maybe just minutes of waiting, felt like an eternity, but before we knew it, the new father, adorned in his hospital attire and holding his new tiny little life, strutted down the hall with all the pride and joy as one would expect. He said, "I want you to meet Hannah!" I couldn't believe it! We were all so sure it would be a boy.

My first thoughts were of my daughter and how close that she and Hannah would be in age. Now there weren't just the hopes that *my* two daughters would be close friends, but that all three girls would be the best of friends. God showed us that not only are His plans truly perfect but that He has a really good sense of humor also!

It was four days later when I gave birth to my daughter. She came rather unexpectedly two weeks early, but as a nice surprise on my sister's own due date. It was a little disappointing not to be able to have my sister there with me during this birth. But I took comfort in the fact that I knew her heart was there with me and she was snuggled next to her own new little life, anxiously waiting for mine to arrive.

CHAPTER 19

During a recent funeral I attended, the pastor included these words in the eulogy, "A Christian's life on earth is the worst that we will ever experience, but for those who do not know the Lord, this life, will be the best there is to offer." My first reaction was to think how sad I felt for those who do not know the Lord; that they had no hope to really cling to, no strength to really rely on and no reassurance of a better life after death. Then, I realized, after putting a lot of thought into it, how truly sad it could be for us Christians as well.

"Give all diligence, add to your faith virtue, to virtue knowledge, to knowledge self-control, to self-control perseverance, to perseverance godliness, to godliness brotherly kindness, and to brotherly kindness love. For if these things are yours abound, you will be neither barren nor unfruitful in the knowledge of our Lord Jesus Christ. For he who lacks these things is shortsighted, even to blindness, and has forgotten that he was cleansed from his old sins." 2 Peter 1:5-9 (Spirit Filled Life Bible). God has made it quite clear what He expects from us as Christians, the rewards when we are obedient and the sufferings when we are not.

God doesn't promise to make life easy for us, but He does expect us to use it to the fullest. He expects us to faithfully lean on Him when times are tough and to make our lives a living example of His love and grace so that, through it all, others may come to know Him. God did not intend for life to be about receiving, achieving or impressing, He intended it to be about giving, sharing and loving. When we are out of step with Him, we lose the rewards of favor with Him, we lose the ability to grow in Him and we miss the opportunities to be that living example for Him.

For those of us Christians who have found ourselves in that very situation, we lose sight of the true calling of God and begin to put our treasures in the things of this world. In effect, we risk a life of no rewards, a life of bearing no fruit and a life of happiness built on sinking sand. But there is hope, because God is forgiving and merciful. It is His desire to bring all of His children back to a full and complete commitment to Him. And only He knows best how to make that happen.

I wasted too much of the life God had given me on the things that did not even matter. My concerns and worries were of this world and not of our heavenly world. I had been blessed with a wonderful life in the care of a loving and godly family. Yet, I failed to treasure that life and to live up to God's intentions for it. It wasn't until I had to witness the trauma my sister went through I was able to renew my relationship with God and come back to a full and complete commitment to Him.

God quickly helped me to realize His intentions for my own life and the blessings He had enriched me with from the very beginning. As a young child and even as a young adult, I never considered myself to possess anything, which would set me apart from others. I never felt gifted. I never felt special. And as I'm sure with most people who struggle with insecurity, there had always been the secret fantasy of making something special out of my life. I dreamed of being a famous actress or a famous singer or being the most popular girl in school.

But it was always just a fantasy of being someone special, convinced of a lifetime of nothingness. Through my sister though, God opened up my eyes to remind me of how special I am to Him and the blessings He desires for me in my own life. God gives each of us special gifts and when we are where God wants us to be, they are as clear to you and me as the nose on our face.

I truly believe that God has a purpose for every person, every event, every situation, and every relationship. God has His mighty hand in everything. He knows all and sees all and plans all. And to bring about His purpose, He uses particular people, particular events, particular situations and particular relationships to make it happen. There is no doubt in my mind that my sister was part of His plans for me. In my own turmoil, she always served as my encourager, supporter and strength. In her turmoil, she served as my earthly angel.

Through all of her tests and through all of the tragedies she experienced, she still found peace. Through all of her depression, she still found joy. Through all of her own experiences, I had seen the rewards of faith, joy and peace and, as a result, was finally able to understand God's intentions for not just my life, but all of our lives. I realized our feelings and needs should be inconsequential. We should desire to meet the physical and emotional needs of others to be that living example of God's unconditional love. And God blesses each of us with our own special gifts to further enable that ultimate desire.

God has given me a gift with words. I never imagined I had the talent or even the inclination to write, but I suddenly found a need and an excitement about putting my thoughts and feelings on paper. I enjoyed bringing the different words together to somehow convey an idea or a character. I enjoyed creating drama that left readers on the edge of their seat. And I enjoyed inventing stories that brought laughter to my children's lives. I realized that this was truly a gift from God and with this realization came responsibility.

God had given me something special and now I was going to use it to bring glory to His name. I know I may never be a famous actress, or singer or even a famous writer, but those are no longer my fantasies. My fantasies involve very different things. I fantasize that somehow through my writing I can bring comfort to those hurting, that I can be an encourager to those who are struggling, that I can bring hope to those who feel hopeless and bring laughter to those who need enrichment. And through it all being an example of God's comforting, encouraging, hopeful and caring hands that bring such joy to all of those who accept Him.

I wrote this book partly as a tribute to my sister to show her how much I appreciate her and what a tremendous inspiration she is to me. However, my ultimate desire was to share with others, through my own failings, the miracle and joy that God intends for life to be. Not only for you, but for others as well. God taught me how precious life was and how important it is to share that preciousness with others. We never know through what life's trials and tragedies will serve as an opportunity to be a godly example to others. God never puts us through anything that we cannot handle. But it's always for His divine purpose.

Whether it's for your own personal spiritual growth, or for the growth of others, God has a plan in mind. As distressing and sometimes, difficult as our situation was at moments, my sister and I are each better for it; lives have been touched, lives have been changed, relationships have been strengthened. I encourage you to live life as God intended it. Give a full and complete commitment to God and He will enlighten you with a peace and an understanding beyond your imagination. The hopes and dreams that were of this world will change to hopes and dreams of God. And then there will be the desire to give of yourself, your talents and your resources to be a living example of Him, allowing you the opportunity to be someone's earthly angel.

* * *